#MY BRAND **tweet** Book01

A Practical Approach to Building Your Personal Brand - 140 Characters at a Time

By Laura Lowell
Foreword by Dan Schwabel

E-mail: info@thinkaha.com
20660 Stevens Creek Blvd., Suite 210,
Cupertino, CA 95014

Published by *THiNKaha*®, a Happy About® imprint
20660 Stevens Creek Blvd., Suite 210, Cupertino, CA 95014
http://thinkaha.com

First Printing: May 2011
Paperback ISBN: 978-1-61699-054-1 (1-61699-054-6)
eBook ISBN: 978-1-61699-055-8 (1-61699-055-4)
Place of Publication: Silicon Valley, California, USA
Paperback Library of Congress Number: 2011928300

Dedication

To my daughters, Taylor and Riley:
Be true to yourselves and your life will
be nothing less than phenomenal.

Acknowledgments

To Rajesh Setty *@RajSetty* for having the idea.

To Mitchell *@HappyAbout* and the team for getting it done.

To Pam Fox Rollin *@PamFR* for making Twitter real for me.

To Rick for giving me time to write it.

To you for reading it.

Why Did I Write This Book?

The idea of "personal branding" has taken on a life of it's own.

Social media and Twitter have changed the world as we know it.

The combination of the two is arguably the most powerful platform you have for building your career.

You must manage #MyBrand or you will lose control of one of your most valuable assets.

Your career will evolve over time taking you from one job, career, industry to another; #MyBrand is the foundation.

I keep getting asked the same questions over and over, so I figured I should write the answers down.

Laura Lowell, *@LauraLowell*
http://lauralowell.com/mybrand

A Practical Approach to Building Your Personal Brand - 140 Characters at a Time

Contents

Foreword by Dan Schwabel

Personal branding is a celebration of who you are and if you want to be successful in your career, make your brand your life!

Dan Schwabel
(*@DanSchwabel*)

into branch
spring out from
branching off the high
business is branching out all o

¹**brand** \'brand\ *n* **1** : a burnt o
a : a mark made by burning
ship, maker, or quality **b** :
ilar purposes : TRADEMARK
criminals with a hot iron
b : a particular
: a class of goods iden

Section I

What Is #MyBrand?

Personal branding has taken on a life of its own. Before creating #MyBrand, it is vital to understand what you mean, what the market thinks you mean, and where the gaps are.

1

Not everyone believes in personal branding; brands are for corps. and products. What are you if not the product of your experiences?

2

Instead of marketing a product or service, #MyBrand promotes a person to a recruiter, hiring manager or prospective client.

3

A brand is a promise you make—a promise of value, consistency, and expectations.

4

#MyBrand is not a cool logo, catchy tagline, celebrity, or multi-million dollar ad campaign—it's you and what you stand for.

5

To build your brand, you must stand for something that is uniquely you, and sets you apart while moving your customers ahead.

6

Be honest with yourself and don't let other people sway you from your priorities, goals and dreams.

7

Value is not something you define, it is something your customers define and you deliver.

8

In real estate, it's all about location, location, location...in branding it's all about consistency, consistency, consistency.

9

Consistency is how you prove your value and deliver on expectations.

10

You can mess up once or twice, but by the third time what is consistent is that you messed up.

11

The first impression isn't always the most important; think about what happens before they know you.

12

Every interaction from email, voicemail, tweets, FB posts (even your online family videos) are part of #MyBrand.

13

Your personal and professional lives are visible and connected online, make sure you're proud of what people can and will see.

14

Since #MyBrand is being created with or without you, you need to actively participate and give them something positive to talk about.

15

#MyBrand is about who you are—
your experience, expertise, and
passion—not what you do.

16

What you're good at and what you
enjoy may not be what you expect—
look beyond the obvious to find your
true strengths.

17

What brings you joy and happiness, what is your passion, include these in #MyBrand so it brings you more of what you love.

18

Combine what you're good at, with what you love and make it the foundation of #MyBrand.

19

Remember to focus on what you're good at and what you love to do—chances are you will do it well and enjoy the process.

20

#MyBrand influences purchases, referrals and your success—make it a no-brainer for people to it.

21

No one ever succeeded by playing it safe; where there are risks, there are rewards.

Section II

The Content of #MyBrand

Whenever you build something, you need to know what it will look like at the end. Then you can make a plan for how to build it.

22

Have a clear objective for #MyBrand, know your purpose and set your sights on the career you ultimately want (not what you currently have).

23

You need to know what you're trying to accomplish in order to make intelligent decisions that move you towards your career goal.

24

Align your objectives with your longer term personal and professional vision.

25

Start with what you want—a promotion, a raise, to change industries, start your own business, establish yourself as an expert.

26

If you could do anything to earn a living what would it be? If you're not doing that, why not?

27

If you can only accomplish one thing this year with #MyBrand, what would it be?

28

What do you expect as a result of #MyBrand in 1, 3 or 5 years?

29

#MyBrand has a strategy
because you can't afford
to create your brand
by accident!

30

#MyBrand lies at the intersection of your audience needs, your expertise and your passion.

31

Who is your audience—your boss,
future clients, prospective employers?
They want to know why #MyBrand
is different.

32

Get to know who #MyBrand is
targeting and they will tell you what
they need to know.

33

What problem is your audience trying to solve—#MyBrand better solve it.

34

What's important to your audience— understand why and you're half way there.

35

Create a demographic profile of your audience—describe them in detail so you have a clear picture of who they are.

36

Detailed demographics include information like age, sex, location... anything that helps you describe your audience.

37

Psychographics are the fundamental need or problem they are trying to solve and the reason for it.

38

Psychographic profiles explain the what and why—look for buying behaviors, emotional connections, social or business affiliations.

39

Prioritize what you do based on what your audience cares about, if they don't care about it, don't do it.

40

Where do they go for information?
Blogs, magazines, conferences,
trade associations—find them
and join them.

41

Online & offline sources, industry
leaders, and communities
are key influencers that need
to be understood.

42

Go to the source and learn about what your audience is learning.

43

Listen to your audience, learn the culture of the group, then speak their language and you will be heard.

44

Research shows the most
important elements of
#MyBrand are personal
presence, speaking ability
and the content you create.

(IMG, 2009)

Section III

How To Build #MyBrand

Objectives and strategies are necessary but not sufficient. You need detailed, actionable tactics to accomplish your objectives.

45

When someone wants to hire #MyBrand be clear about what you will do and how it will benefit them.

46

Everyone is an expert at something—look at what you know, and what you are known for.

47

Evaluate your experience—personal and professional—use the common themes to help build #MyBrand.

48

Everyone is good at something— what do you like to do, what is your big idea?

49

If you are passionate about something you are more likely to do it, and do it well.

50

Americans spend > 30% of their time working; life is too short to spend time on things you don't like & don't make you happy. (BLS, 2009)

51

Do a few things really well and prove to people that #MyBrand has value and delivers on what you promise.

52

Define your niche, be a small fish in a big pond OR be the big fish in a small pond, the choice is yours.

53

Once you define your niche, claim it, own it and protect your position.

54

Stand alone and you will stand out; but stand fast because it can be lonely.

55

#MyBrand needs a value proposition that puts you in context of the competition.

56

Your value proposition is your UNIQUE offering—what customers, employers, and partners can expect from EVERY interaction with you.

57

Who or what is your competition—other people, services, or the dreaded "do nothing?"

58

#MyBrand offers [something] to enable [someone] to do [something] better than the competition.

59

Brand positioning means

knowing your relative

strengths and weaknesses

and putting yourself

in context.

60

What is the single most important thing #MyBrand promises to deliver to your audience?

61

How do you want people to FEEL about #MyBrand after interacting with you?

62

If #MyBrand was a car, what kind would it be and why? Are you a eco-friendly hybrid, a classic with style, or an outdoor loving SUV?

63

What is the theme song for #MyBrand? Have your audience sing along with you.

64

Think about specific personality traits you want clients, employers, and partners to use to describe #MyBrand.

65

Identify 4-5 adjectives that you want your audience to use when they describe you to someone—use these in #MyBrand.

66

Research shows that the most important attributes of #MyBrand are Honesty, Authenticity and Expertise. (IMG, 2009)

67

#MyBrand promise + personality is what will make your personal brand POP!

68

Your promise is a combination of your ideas, messages, copy, creative and campaigns you use to communicate to your audience.

69

#MyBrand personality is a combination of your tone, language, sense of humor and style your audience sees from you.

70

Are you: Authentic, Creative,

Innovative, Approachable,

Trustworthy, Trendy, Cool,

Desirable, Reliable, Relevant,

Honest, Flexible, Unique?

71

Your promise and personality should drive your personal brand identity.

72

Is #MyBrand promise being consistently communicated?

73

Authenticity is ranked as one of the top elements of #MyBrand, but it's just a fancy way of saying "be true to yourself."

74

Say "Thanks" and mean it—everyone likes someone who is polite, respectful and appreciative.

75

Business is serious business, but there is still room for humor and a well-placed joke.

76

Be honest—with yourself and your audience—even little white lies will come back to haunt you (online everything lives forever).

Section IV

The Mechanics of #MyBrand

My grandmother used to say
"The devil is in the details".
I think she was right.

77

#MyBrand identity combines words, images, colors, and other elements to convey the idea behind your personal brand.

78

Brand design is the aesthetic that communicates the underlying message and personality of the brand.

79

Content is the substance of your business that your audience will find valuable.

80

Words matter—subtle nuances can mean the difference between connecting with and pissing off your audience.

81

Messages are the ideas your brand conveys—consistently overtime, in everything you do.

82

Copy are the unique words used to communicate the message in specific vehicles like ads, webpages, direct mail, PR....

83

Copy should reflect current industry trends, cultural icons and social phenomena. Messages should focus on a single core idea.

84

Just because you're tired of the message doesn't mean your audience is—they haven't seen it a hundred times (yet).

85

Are your messages being clearly conveyed in ALL communications?

86

Do your actions support the promise of #MyBrand?

87

What's in a name? Your name, your company name, a fanciful name, a made-up name, a descriptive name—they all have a place.

88

Make sure the name you choose for #MyBrand is actually yours to use; verify trademarks, URLs and common law usage.

89

A good tagline is the strongest, shortest and simplest expression of #MyBrand.

90

A picture is worth 1,000 words, but a good logo can be worth millions of dollars.

91

Every color is imbued with a subconscious meaning; blue is trustworthy, green is peaceful, yellow is happy, red is exciting.

92

Typyography is the art of arranging type including the font type, point size, line length, line spacing, and even space between letters.

93

Images explain #MyBrand; realistic photos, abstract animation, stark illustrations or whatever your creative mind can come up with.

94

Test #MyBrand with your audience—ask them questions and listen to what they say. You need to learn enough to avoid a silly mistake.

Section V

Getting #MyBrand Out There

Understand the tools, use them to communicate #MyBrand to your audience, and get them to hire you, promote you, refer you....

95

If it isn't integrated across your entire business...#MyBrand won't work.

96

#MyBrand strategy is a process that allows you to concentrate limited resources on your greatest opportunities.

97

Build your marketing plan based on a set of specific actions needed to successfully implement your marketing strategy.

98

Awareness means that people know about #MyBrand—think "eyes and ears"—they have seen or heard about you.

99

The goal of #MyBrand is to generate demand for your services—get them to call, click or visit.

100

Your audience can't demand your services if they don't know you exist, so make sure they know you're out there.

101

Once they know #MyBrand and they want what you have, make it easy-peasy for them to say YES.

102

Leads must be converted; meaning prospects become clients, and interviews become offers.

103

Invest in strategic relationships to increase awareness among their network and add credibility to #MyBrand.

104

Who has influence among your audience? Get to know them, be their friend and see how you can help them and they will return the favor.

105

Don't "kiss up" or pretend to want to help; add value, give advice, share freely and openly. It will come back to you tenfold.

106

Think about the DEPTH and BREADTH of #MyBrand—map against target vertical or horizontal— then flip it upside down.

107

Make sure it is known that you are an expert; it isn't bragging if you can back it up (even if it is bragging, a little goes along way).

108

Volunteer when your expertise is needed; it's a great way to build awareness and positive perceptions of #MyBrand (as well as referrals).

109

Find opportunities to share your expertise online and offline; but only if you really mean it 'cuz otherwise people can tell.

110

Leverage your networks, but more importantly, your friends networks to connect beyond your immediate circle and expand your reach.

111

If you only talk to yourself and your existing circle, you're not going to grow; join new groups online AND offline.

112

Online groups are great—LinkedIn Groups, Answers, FaceBook Groups, Twitter #chats.

113

Offline groups and networking events still need to be a fundamental part of your marketing strategy to grow #MyBrand.

114

Don't talk for the sake of talking; a little spin on what Mom always said "If you can't say anything USEFUL don't say anything at all."

115

If #MyBrand has something that can help someone else, then jump in and HELP (without expecting anything in return).

116

Build a platform for #MyBrand with blogs, articles, books, speaking, webcasts—it makes it easier for your audience to find you.

117

Track industry & vertical blogs to keep up with the latest in your field, comment to increase exposure and awareness of #MyBrand.

118

Comment on blogs with relevant, useful and insightful ideas that add something; don't just reiterate, it makes you look dumb.

119

To give is to receive;
reference other people
in your blog—it's a nice
complement, builds goodwill
and collaboration.

120

Go beyond yourself—who, what, where, when and how you can grow #MyBrand can not be limited to your ideas only.

121

Use the right tools for promoting #MyBrand—not everyone is a Twitoholic—but if your audience is then it's a great place for you.

122

All roads lead to #MyBrand's website—it is your "plan of record" and should feed other online venues like FB, T, LI....

123

SEO is a requirement IF #MyBrand is online search dependent—you need to be on top or they won't know you exist.

124

If #MyBrand is referral dependent—focus on your referral sources and make them LOVE you.

125

Only blog if you like to write; otherwise it will work against you when your latest post is 3 months old.

126

Publish articles that reinforce your expertise; they add credibility, improve SEO, and are great assets to share with new contacts.

127

Increasing your online and offline is critical but ONLY if you're visible among your audience—recruiters, employeers, or clients.

128

Co-marketing is a made up terms for "you scratch my back and I'll scratch yours;" it's worked for hundreds of years and still does.

129

Media coverage is great for your ego; but more often than not, it doesn't generate referrals, revenue or repeat clients.

130

Your personal presence is the most important vehicle to get #MyBrand out there. (IMG 2009)

131

Start a conversation...an actual dialogue with another person about something important to them (I repeat...important to THEM).

132

Be transparent about the motivation behind #MyBrand; you want recruiters, employers and clients to know why you do what you do.

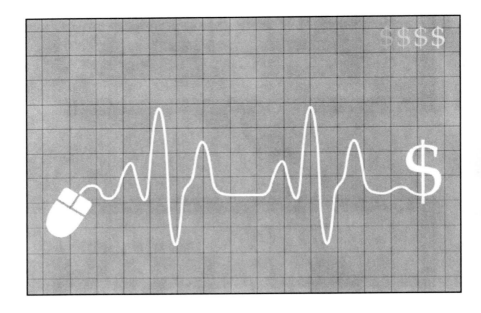

Section VI

Keeping #MyBrand Alive

Keeping #MyBrand current and relevant is one of the most important investments (in yourself, your career, and your business) you will ever make.

133

Take action everyday to nurture #MyBrand; it takes time to build a garden, but left untended, it will be just a big tangle of weeds.

134

Try something NEW every day; meet a new person, try a new networking site, watch a new webinar, read a new book.

135

Don't be afraid to reinvent yourself; consider it a make-over, a refresh of the original... think "New and Improved."

136

Allow #MyBrand to evolve
organically; in the right environment
a little seed of an idea can grown and
morphy into a beautiful flower.

137

Challenge #MyBrand; ask your
colleagues, peers and associates for
feedback especially the unpleasant
kind, it's the most useful.

138

Embrace your mistakes; it means you're trying new things, experimenting and learning (just don't make them more than once).

139

Realize that social media is your way to be heard; get on it, work in it, embrace it, use it (strategically), but DON'T ignore it.

140

Social equity, not financial

equity, is how #MyBrand

is ultimately valued;

it is a priceless asset

not to be wasted.

Appendix A: Folks to Follow

Beverly Macy, *@BeverlyMacy*

Chad Levitt, *@ChadALevitt*

Charles Brown, *@CharBrown*

Chris Brogan, *@ChrisBrogan*

Dan Schawbel, *@DanSchawbel*

Dave Saunders, *@DaveSaunders*

David Sandusky, *@DavidSandusky*

Dr. Fern Kazlow, *@DrFernKazlow*

Gillian Kelly, *@Gillian_Kelly*

Hajj Flemings, *@HajjFlemings*

Jacob Share, *@JacobShare*

Jason Alba, *@JasonAlba*

Jeffrey Blake, *@Jeffrey_Blake*

Jun Loayza, *@JunLoayza*

Katie Konrath, *@KatieKonrath*

Kirsten Dixson, *@KirstenDixson*

Krishna De, *@KrishnaDe*

Liz Lynch, *@Liz_Lynch*

Louise Mowbray, *@LouiseMowbray*

Meg Guiseppi, *@MegGuiseppi*

Monica O'Brien, *@MonicaObrien*

Ola Rynge, *@Rynge*

Rob Cuesta, *@RobCuesta*

Rob Frankel, *@brandingexpert*

Roger C. Parker, *@Rogercparker*

Scott Scanlon, *@ScottScanlon*

Seth Godin, *@ThisIsSethsBlog*

Tessa Faber, *@MakingSense*

Tom Peters, *@tom_peters*

Trace Cohen & Pete Kistler's Brand-Yourself, *@Brandyourself*

Warren Whitlock, *@WarrenWhitlock*

Wendy Marx, *@WendyMarx*

William Arruda, *@WilliamArruda*

Appendix B: Lists to Track

Marketing by Danny Sullivan
http://twitter.com/#!/dannysullivan/marketing

500 Elite Follows by *@DaviesWriter*
http://twitter.com/#!/DaviesWriter/vip-500-elite-follows

Thought Leaders by Josh Weinberger
http://twitter.com/#!/kitson/thought-leaders

Social Media Smarties by Susan Beebe
http://twitter.com/#!/susanbeebe/social-media-smarties

Word Nerds by Rebecca Woodhead
http://listorious.com/rebeccawoodhead/word-nerds

The Rocket List by Chris Perry
http://twitter.com/#!/CareerRocketeer/the-rocket-list

Job Search Experts by Susan P. Joyce
http://twitter.com/#!/JobHuntOrg/job-search-experts

Personal Branding by Mohammed al Taee
http://twitter.com/#!/MAltaee/personal-branding

Innovation by Braden Kelly
http://twitter.com/#!/innovate/innovation

Entrepreneur by Chuck Blakeman
http://twitter.com/#!/ChuckBlakeman/entrepreneur

Social Media Marketing by Sam Wee
http://twitter.com/#!/swee06840/social-media-marketing

Career Coaches/Job Search by Jennifer McClure
http://twitter.com/#!/CincyRecruiter/career-coaches-job-search

Small Biz by John Jantsch
http://twitter.com/#!/ducttape/smallbiz

Community by Recruiting Blogs
http://twitter.com/#!/RecruitingBlogs/community

Appendix C: Chats to Check Out

#ASMChat Spanish monthly chat where you'll find everything about Social Media: tips, experiences, Q&A and so. Meet people from different countries of (Latin America) the last Tuesday of each month. See you there!

#BeTheOne A monthly chat about inspiring people to make a difference through personal leadership that infuses integrity, dignity and character.

#brandchat A discussion between experts, strategists, and those interested in learning more about personal and business brand management.

#careerchat Got career issues? Discuss them here! Watch for weekly topics. All questions welcome.

#CareerSavvy Want to find, land, and succeed in your career? Join the Vestiigo.com team for this weekly chat covering important career topics.

#CareerSuccess Career Success Radio - on BlogTalkRadio.

#GenYJobs A bi-weekly hour chat for young professionals seeking support and guidance in today's challenging job arena.

#GetMoreClients Weekly chat about branding, marketing and business-building strategies so you can get more clients, get noticed, hired & paid what you're worth!

#hmchat Professional women share on biz, lifestyle, and personal inspiration. Each chat is centered around our quarterly series.

#ideachat Focused on ideas, the process of ideation and making ideas happen. A salon of some of the most innovative thinkers on Twitter. Every month, a particular book relevant to topic and its author are invited to share ideas.

#ideaparty An idea party is where friends—or even total strangers—gather to tell their wishes and the obstacles that might be keeping them from achieving them. Think of it as "Speed Networking."

#jobhuntchat Weekly chat for job seekers & experts.

#LeadershipChat A lively discussion every Tuesday night for Leaders and those aspiring to become leaders.

#LeadFromWithin Weekly chat to discuss heart-driven, values-aligned leadership.

#LinkedinChat A weekly chat for people who have questions and/or advice on how to use LinkedIn effectively.

#SmallBizChat Helpful tips and advice geared toward small business startups and those that have been in business for less than five years. We host a different guest & questions each week. Follow *@SmallBizChat* to find details each week.

#SMBiz Open chat session where small businesses of every kind can meet, network and ask all kinds of questions in any of the aforementioned areas.

#wgbiz A monthly Twitter chat by, for and of women in business. It extends the Women Grow Business blog community.

A Practical Approach to Building Your Personal Brand - 140 Characters at a Tim

About the Author

Laura Lowell has drawn on her years of experience building some of the world's biggest brands including HP, Intel and IBM where she learned the fine art of branding from the ground up. She has condensed everything she learned into the pages of *#MyBrand tweet.*

Laura founded Impact Marketing Group in 2005. Her first book, *42 Rules for Marketing,* was an Amazon.com bestseller. Her second book, *42 Rules for Working Moms*, combined her expertise and her passion, and was featured on Oprah & Friends Radio, *The Peter Walsh Show.*

A degree in International Relations prepared her for work assignments in Hong Kong and London, after which she received her MBA from UC Berkeley, Haas School of Business with an emphasis on marketing and entrepreneurship. Wanting to expose her children to her love of all things "global," Laura and her family recently spent a year living in Malaga, Spain.

Laura has been featured on Oprah & Friends, ABC, The Huffington Post, and more. She is also an active blogger writing on marketing, personal branding, and social media in "The Rules...According to You." A dynamic speaker, Laura has been a keynote speaker at conferences around the world.

Other Books in the THiNKaha Series

The THiNKaha book series is for thinking adults who lack the time or desire to read long books, but want to improve themselves with knowledge of the most up-to-date subjects. THiNKaha is a leader in timely, cutting-edge books and mobile applications from relevant experts that provide valuable information in a fun, Twitter-brief format for a fast-paced world.

They are available online at http://thinkaha.com or at other online and physical bookstores.

1. *#BOOK TITLE tweet Book01:* 140 Bite-Sized Ideas for Compelling Article, Book, and Event Titles by Roger C. Parker

2. *#COACHING tweet Book01:* 140 Bite-Sized Insights On Making A Difference Through Executive Coaching by Sterling Lanier

3. *#CONTENT MARKETING tweet Book01:* 140 Bite-Sized Ideas to Create and Market Compelling Content by Ambal Balakrishnan

4. *#CORPORATE CULTURE tweet Book01:* 140 Bite-Sized Ideas to Help You Create a High Performing, Values Aligned Workplace that Employees LOVE by S. Chris Edmonds

5. *#CROWDSOURCING tweet Book01:* 140 Bite-Sized Ideas to Tap into the Wisdom of the Crowd by Kiruba Shankar and Mitchell Levy

6. *#DEATHtweet Book01:* A Well-Lived Life through 140 Perspectives on Death and Its Teachings by Timothy Tosta

7. *#DEATH tweet Book02:* 140 Perspectives on Being a Supportive Witness to the End of Life by Timothy Tosta

8. *#DIVERSITYtweet Book01:* Embracing the Growing Diversity in Our World by Deepika Bajaj

9. *#DREAMtweet Book01:* Inspirational Nuggets of Wisdom from a Rock and Roll Guru to Help You Live Your Dreams by Joe Heuer

10. *#ENTRYLEVELtweet Book01:* Taking Your Career from Classroom to Cubicle by Heather R. Huhman

11. *#ENTRY LEVEL tweet Book02:* Inspiration for New Professionals by Christine Ruff and Lori Ruff

12. *#IT OPERATIONS MANAGEMENT tweet Book01:* Managing Your IT Infrastructure in The Age of Complexity by Peter Spielvogel, Jon Haworth, Sonja Hickey

13. *#JOBSEARCHtweet Book01:* 140 Job Search Nuggets for Managing Your Career and Landing Your Dream Job by Barbara Safani

CPSIA information can be obtained at www.ICGtesting.com
Printed in the USA

268610BV00001B/1/P